The Ride of Pride

Written by

**Sonya Johnson, Ph.D. and
Yvonne Johnson, Ph.D.**

AuthorHouse™
1663 Liberty Drive
Bloomington, IN 47403
www.authorhouse.com
Phone: 1 (800) 839-8640

Published by AuthorHouse 03/08/2016

ISBN: 978-1-5049-7904-7 (sc)
ISBN: 978-1-5049-7905-4 (e)

Library of Congress Control Number: 2016902868

Print information available on the last page.

Any people depicted in stock imagery provided by Thinkstock are models,
and such images are being used for illustrative purposes only.
Certain stock imagery © Thinkstock.

This book is printed on acid-free paper.

Because of the dynamic nature of the Internet, any web addresses or links contained in this book may have changed
since publication and may no longer be valid. The views expressed in this work are solely those of the author and do
not necessarily reflect the views of the publisher, and the publisher hereby disclaims any responsibility for them.

authorHOUSE®

Jaylen Anderson is playing basketball with his friends when his mother calls him in to do his homework.

Shortly after Jaylen starts his homework, Mrs. Anderson can hear the sound of video games coming from his room. She knocks on his door.

Mrs. Anderson asks,--"Have you finished your homework already?". "Yes Ma'am" he answers. "What was your homework assignment?" Mrs. Anderson asks. "My teacher, Mrs. Johnson, asked us to write about a black inventor," Jaylen replies. "May I see your report?" Mrs. Anderson asks. Jaylen hands his mother his report. She looks at the report then shows it to Mr. Anderson. Mr. Anderson studies the report briefly, and then hands it back to Jaylen.

Later that night Mr. and Mrs. Anderson discussed Jaylen's school performance. "He's not a bad student", they agree, " he's getting good grades but he could do much better if he spent more time on his work".

"We need a way to motivate him," Mrs. Anderson says. "I have an idea", Mr. Anderson says. The next night Jaylen notices his father busy working at his desk with the computer and stacks of books.

"What is he working on?" Jaylen asks his mother, "Oh--he's just doing some homework," Mrs. Anderson says jokingly.

The next morning while Jaylen is getting ready for school his mother is ironing his clothes. "See the ironing board that your mother is using?" Mr. Anderson asks-"The **ironing board** was invented by **Sarah Boone**, a black woman, in 1892," checking his notepad.

After Mrs. Anderson finished ironing his clothes, Jaylen continues to get dressed. While Jaylen was putting on his shoes, Mr. Anderson says," The process of making shoes was automated by the invention of a black man, **A. R. Cooper,** in 1899. Before then shoes were made by hand-- this was a very slow process."

"Be sure to eat your breakfast before you go". Mrs. Anderson reminds Jaylen, "It's the most important meal of the day they say."

Jaylen opens the refrigerator to get milk for his cereal. Mr. Anderson says, "Did you know that **John Standard,** a black man, received a patent for an improved **refrigerator** design in 1891?"

"Don't catch the bus from school this afternoon, I'll pick you up at 3:30 p.m.," Mr. Anderson tells Jaylen.

That afternoon, Mr. Anderson arrives at the school to pick up Jaylen.

Jaylen checks his watch as he gets into the car.

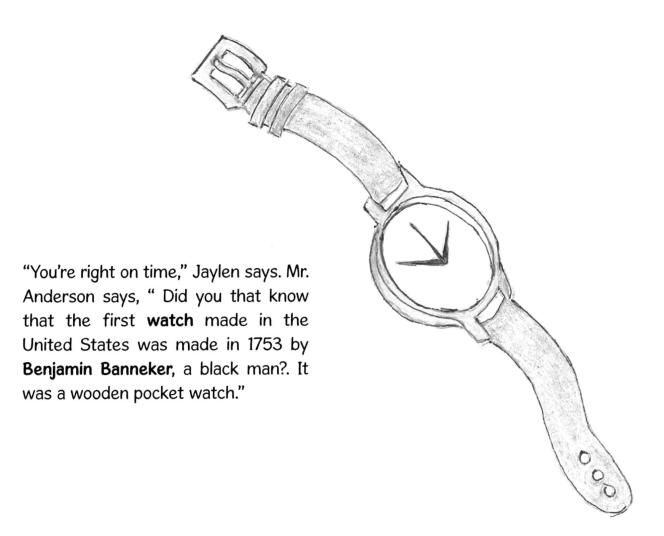

"You're right on time," Jaylen says. Mr. Anderson says, " Did you that know that the first **watch** made in the United States was made in 1753 by **Benjamin Banneker,** a black man?. It was a wooden pocket watch."

When they get home the phone was ringing. It was Mrs. Anderson. "She has to work late today. She wants us to bring her a sandwich." Mr. Anderson says. Mr. Anderson says to Jaylen, " The research of Dr. Shirley Ann Jackson, a black theoretical physicist, enabled others to invent the portable fax, touch tone telephone, caller ID, and call waiting."

While driving to take Mrs. Anderson a sandwich, Mr. Anderson says to Jaylen, "**Richard B. Spikes** received a patent for the **Automatic Gear Shift** in 1932."

They stopped to get a sandwich, then went to the hospital where Mrs. Anderson is a nurse. When they reached the hospital they had to take the elevator since Mrs. Anderson works on the third floor. As they are waiting for the elevator, Mr. Anderson checks his notepad again, then tells Jaylen that **Alexander Miles**, a black man received a patent for the **electric elevator** in 1877.

Mr. Anderson points to a security camera and tells Jaylen that **Marie Van Brittan Brown**, a black women, invented the **Home Security System** utilizing television surveillance in 1969

As they are walking down the hall to meet Mrs. Anderson, Mr. Anderson tells Jaylen that black men and women have made many contributions in the field of medicine-- glancing at his notepad from time to time.

The **disposable needle** was invented by **Phil Brooks in 1974.**

Dr. Charles Drew's work with blood plasma made **Blood Transfusions** possible. Thousands of lives have been saved by blood transfusions.

Dr. Daniel Hale Williams was a pioneer in **open heart surgery**. He performed the first successful open-heart surgery in the United States.

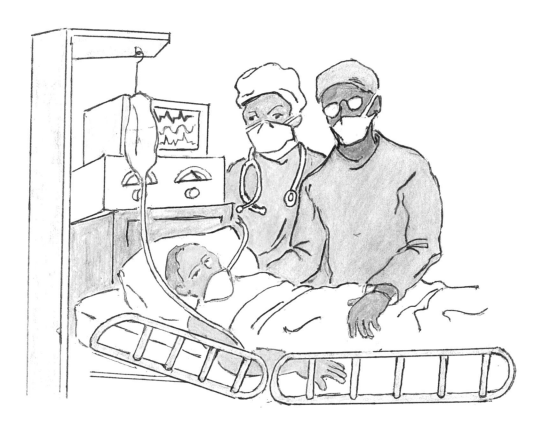

Dr. Ben Carson, Pediatric Neurosurgeon, was the first surgeon to successfully **separate craniopagus twins** (twins joined at the skull).

Dr. Patricia Bath, Opthalmologist, invented procedures that relate to **cataract surgery** and include the **Laserphaco Probe.**

Otis Boykin invented a **control unit for artificial heart stimulators.**

They met Mrs. Anderson and gave her the sandwich.

As they were leaving the hospital Mr. Anderson points out a **fire extinguisher** in the hall. "**Thomas Marshall** received a patent for his improvement to the **fire extinguisher** in 1872," Mr. Anderson says.

Now Jaylen knows why his father is carrying the notepad everywhere, and what his dad's homework was.

"On the way home can we stop to get some school supplies?" Jaylen asks.

They stop at an office supply store where Jaylen buys pencils, notebook paper, and a pencil sharpener.

"The **pencil sharpener** was invented by **John Lee Love**, a black man, in 1897," Mr. Anderson says.

On the way home traffic was very heavy, "Imagine what traffic would be like without traffic lights," says Mr. Anderson, " the **traffic light** was invented by a black man, **Garrett Morgan**, in 1923."

17

When they get home they decided to wait on Mrs. Anderson before eating dinner. Jaylen went to his room and started on his homework. Mrs. Anderson was surprised when she got home to find him getting his homework already--because it is Friday.

During dinner that evening, Jaylen asks his dad if he can use their lawnmower tomorrow to cut Mrs. Brown's lawn. "She says she'll pay me if it's okay with you. I can use the money to buy those tennis shoes I've been saving for," Jaylen says. "Sure you can," Mr. Anderson replies, "and did you know that the **lawnmower** was invented by **John A. Burr,** a black man, in 1899?"

After cutting Mrs. Brown's yard Jaylen comes home tired. "Is the air conditioner on?" he asks--checking the thermostat and air conditioner vents.

Mr. Anderson assures Jaylen that the air conditioner is running. He also tells him that the **air conditioner unit** was invented by **Frederick M. Jones** in 1949, and the **vent** that they blow through was invented by **J.T. Darkins** in 1895, both black men.

That evening at dinner Jaylen tells his parents that he has been thinking about entering the science fair this year. "Will you help me find a project?" he asks. "Of course we will," his father replies.

Mr. and Mrs. Anderson have been noticing that Jaylen comes in from playing basketball without being called, and he's spending a lot more time on his homework than before.

Mr. and Mrs. Anderson are very pleased-- feeling that they have achieved their goal.

APPENDIX

More inventions by black inventors that are common in everyday life.

Automatic Shoe Making Machine-was invented by
Jan Matzeliger in 1883. Patent #274,207

The X-Ray Spectrometer-was invented by **George E. Alcorn** in 1986.
Patent #4,618,380

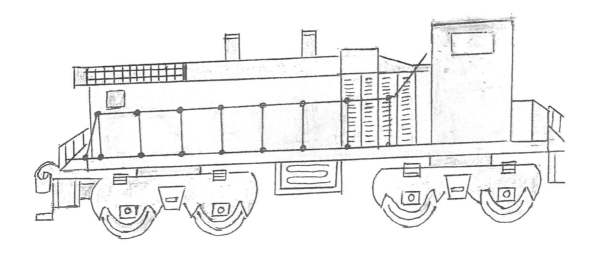

Railway Air Brakes- Invented by **Granville T. Woods** in 1903. This provided the first safe method of stopping trains. Patent #755,825

Auto Car Coupling Device-Invented by **Andrew Beard** in 1897. This device, known as the Jenny Coupler, automatically joined cars by allowing them to bump into each other. Patent #594,059

Railway Telegraphy-Invented by **Granville T. Woods** in 1887. This was train to station communication. Patent #373,383

Refrigeration for Railroad Cars- Invented by **Frederick T. Jones** in 1945.

Mop-Invented by **Thomas N. Stewart** in 1893. Patent #499,402

Dust Pan- Invented by **Lawrence P. Ray** in 1897. Patent #587,607

Peanut Products - George Washington Carver invented hundreds of peanut products.

Air Conditioner Unit- Invented by **Frederick T. Jones** in 1949. Patent #2,475,841

Vent- Invented by **J.T. Darkins** in in 1895. Patent #534,322

The Portable Pencil Sharpener- Invented by **John Lee Love** in 1899. Patent #594,114

Refrigeration for Transport Trucks- Invented by **Frederick T Jones** in 1958.

Horse Shoe- Invented by **James Ricks** in 1885. Patent #338,781

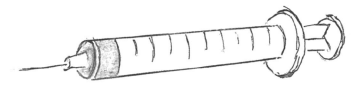

Disposable Needle- Invented by **Phil Brooks** in 1974. Patent #3,802,434

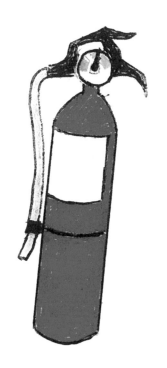

Fire Extinguisher- **Thomas J. Marshall** received a patent for his improved **Fire Extinguisher Design** in 1897. Patent #125,063

Typewriter-Lee Burridge and **Newman P. Marshman** received patents for their innovative **typewriter improvements.**
Lee Burridge and **Newman Marshman** 1896 Great Brittan Patent # 14,288
Lee Burridge- 1897 US Patent #575145 A
Newman P. Marshman- 1898 US Patent #599,397 A

Bicycle Frame- Isaac R. Johnson invented a **folding bicycle frame** in 1899. Patent #634,823

Tricycle - Matthew A. Cherry invented the **tricycle** in 1886. Patent #382,351

Lawn Sprinkler- Joseph Smith invented the **lawn sprinkler** in 1897. Patent #581,785

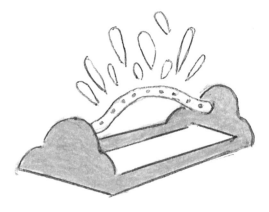

Rolling Pin- Judy W. Reed invented the **rolling pin** in 1864. Patent #305,474

Biscuit Cutter-A.P. Ashbourne invented the **biscuit cutter** in 1875. Patent #170,460

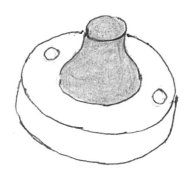

Straightening Comb-Madam C.J. Walker developed many cosmetic and hair products. She received a patent for her improved **Straightening Comb Design** in 1905.

Mail Box-**Paul L. Downing** invented the **street mail box** in 1891. Patent #462,096

29

GAS MASK- Garrett A. Morgan invented the **gas mask** in 1914. Patent #1,090,936

G.T. Sampson invented the **Clothes Dryer** in 1862. Patent #476,416

Refrigerator-J. **Standard** received a patent in 1891 for an **improved refrigerator design**. Patent #455,891

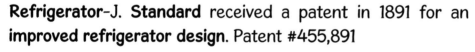

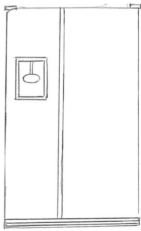

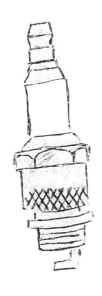

Spark Plug- Edmond Berger invented the **spark plug** in 1839.

Egg Beater-Willie Johnson invented the **egg beater** in 1884. Patent # 292,821

Sugar Refining - Norbert Rillieux improved **sugar refining** with the invention of the **Evaporation Pan System.** The triple evaporation pan system was patented in 1843.

Potato Chip- George Crum invented the **potato chip** originally known as the **Saratoga Chip.** He did not get a patent.

Butter Churn-A.C. Richardson invented the **Butter Churn** in 1891. Patent #446,470

Key Chain- Frederick J. Loudin invented the **key chain** in 1894 Patent #512,308

Light Bulb- Thomas Edison invented the **light bulb,** but **Lewis Howard Latimer** perfected it with the invention of a more durable **carbon filament** in 1882. Patent #252,386

Street Sweeper- Charles B. Brooks invented the U.S. first **self-propelled street sweeper truck** in 1896. Patent #556,711

Super Soaker- Lonnie George Johnson invented the **Super Soaker** in 1982. Patent #5,510,819

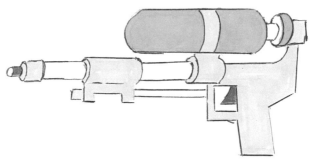

Golf Tee-George Franklin Grant invented the **wooden golf tee** in 1849. Patent #638,920

Security Camera- Marie Van Brittan Brown invented the **home security system** utilizing television surveillance in 1969. Patent #3,482,037

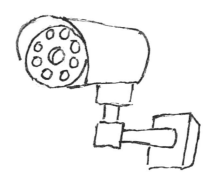

Lawn Mower- John A. Burr invented the **lawn mower** in 1889. Patent #624,749

Ice Cream Scoop-The **ice cream scoop** was invented by **Alfred L. Cralle** in 1897. Patent #576,395

Fountain Pen- The **fountain pen** was invented by **William B. Purvis** in 1890. Patent #419,065

Computer- Mark Dean was an IBM computer scientist. He was one of the original inventors of the IBM personal computer. Mark Dean, Ph.D. holds three of the IBM's original nine PC patents.

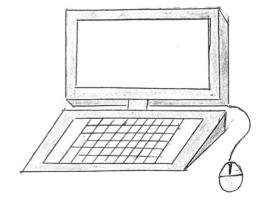

Ben Carson, Pediatric Neurosurgeon, was the first surgeon to successfully **separate craniopagus twins.**

Phone- **Dr. Shirley Ann Jackson's** research enabled others to invent the **portable fax, touch tone telephone, caller ID,** and **call waiting.**

Yvonne

Sonya

Bibliography

Yvonne Johnson, Ph.D. and Sonya Johnson, Ph.D. were born and raised in Memphis, TN. Yvonne received her Bachelor of Arts in History from Clark Atlanta University, her Master of Arts in Teaching from the University of Memphis, and Doctor of Philosophy in Education from Capella University.

Sonya received her Bachelor of Science in Chemistry from Clark Atlanta University, her Master of Arts in Teaching from the University of Memphis, and Doctor of Philosophy in Education from Capella University.

Both Johnson sisters are educators in the Shelby County Schools System.
The Illustrator, Lee E. Johnson, is the father of Yvonne and Sonya.

Who invented the traffic light, the mop, or even the pencil sharpener? Travel with Jaylen as he learns pieces of history. See how his hesitation to complete his homework assignment turns into a life changing learning experience. You and your family can learn the history of several inventions while taking an everyday stroll in the neighborhood.

Yvonne Johnson, Ph.D., and Sonya Johnson, Ph.D. were born and raised in Memphis,TN. Yvonne received her Bachelor of Arts in History from Clark Atlanta University, her Master of Arts in Teaching from the University of Memphis, and Doctor of Philosophy in Education from Capella University. Sonya Johnson, Ph.D. received her Bachelor of Science in Chemistry from Clark Atlanta University, her Master of Arts in Teaching from the University of Memphis, and Doctor of Philosophy in Education from Capella University. Both Johnson sisters work for Shelby County Schools. Their father, Lee Johnson, is the book's Illustrator.

Printed in the United States
By Bookmasters